Mental

Toughness

Excessive Thinking: Be yourself and quickly improve self-esteem using successful habits and meditation A step by step guide to facing life's challenges, managing negative emotions and overcoming adversity with courage and balance

Table of Contents

Furthermore, the transmission, duplication, or reproduction of any of the following work including specific information will be considered an illegal act irrespective of if it is done electronically or in print. This extends to creating a secondary or tertiary copy of the work or a recorded copy and is only allowed with the express written consent from the Publisher. All additional right reserved.

The information in the following pages is broadly considered a truthful and accurate account of facts and as such, any inattention, use, or misuse of the information in question by the reader will render any resulting actions solely under their purview. There are no scenarios in which the publisher or the original author of this work can be in any fashion deemed liable for any hardship or damages that may befall them after undertaking information described herein.

Additionally, the information in the following pages is intended only for informational purposes and should thus be thought of as universal. As befitting its nature, it is presented without assurance regarding its prolonged validity or interim quality. Trademarks that are mentioned are done without written consent and can in no way be considered an endorsement from the trademark holder.

Introduction

Congratulations on downloading *Mental Toughness* and thank you for doing so.

The following chapters will discuss exactly what is mental toughness, how you can achieve and improve your mental toughness, the benefits of having mental toughness, traits and characteristics of a person who has mental toughness. You will also discover how fear and stress interact with mental toughness and how developing your mental toughness can help you deal with these two issues. You will also learn more about setting goals and how mental toughness can help you achieve these goals more effectively and efficiently.

Furthermore, you will learn a great deal about emotional intelligence, including what emotional intelligence is, and when and how to use it. There are many ways in which having a higher level of emotional intelligence can benefit you. You will learn how to develop and use these skills by reading this book, so that by the end it, you will have a comprehensive understanding of what emotional intelligence is and how to hone and utilize these skills to improve your life. There are plenty of books on this subject on the market, thanks again for choosing this one! Every effort was made to ensure it is full of as much useful information as possible. Please enjoy!

Chapter 1: How to Build Mental Strength

Mental strength is not something that you have to be born with. It develops over time due to your life experiences, observations, associations with other people, and other factors that shape who you are. It can develop naturally over time. You do, however, have the ability to control the development of mental strength that you have. You can take steps to actively hone your mental strength skills so that you can perform the tasks that you choose to undertake in your daily life at a high level.

There are a number of techniques that you can use to build mental strength. Some of these techniques included are small one-step actions while others are multi-step processes.

The process of building mental strength takes dedication and practice. The progress and improvements that you will see in your mental toughness will take time and a significant amount of practice. The amount of mental toughness that you develop is dependent on whether you practice these techniques and focus on developing mental toughness for a specific goal with a set date such as joining the police force or becoming a professional athlete, or whether you want to hone your skills by slow and steady progression with the intention of putting them to use over a lifetime.

Take A Long Hard Look at Yourself and Evaluate Who You Are

One exercise that you can do to enhance your mental toughness is to take a good look at who you are, your values, and your beliefs and see if you are living up to those values and beliefs in your daily life. This is part of familiarizing yourself with yourself. Most people believe that they know themselves, but many are surprised to find out that they might be wrong. You may have done things a certain way for so long that you have never thought about why you are doing them; they are just habits. You could have gotten them from your parents when you were young, watching other people, television, and more. You may believe that these actions and thoughts say a lot about you and your values, but they may not say as much as you believe. This is why it is a good idea to take a long hard look at yourself and evaluate who you are. You may find out that you are a little different than you originally thought you were.

Examine things about yourself such as your personality. What are some of your character traits? What is your personality like to you? What do the people around you think of your personality? Where do the answers to the last two questions differ? Examine what emotions you need to control and what emotions you need to show more of and develop further.

Your values and beliefs

Take the time to identify and examine your core values and beliefs. What are they? Be as specific as possible and jot them down. After writing down your values and beliefs, it is a tie for you to try to access why these are your core values and beliefs. Is it because they were your parents' values and beliefs that were handed down to you? Are they the same values and beliefs that you had when you were a child? If so, do they still apply to your life today? Really take the time to think about it so that you can assess whether these values are a good thing for you to hold on to and aspire to as you try to achieve your goals.

Don't let old values and beliefs keep you from achieving your current goals. Many of the values that you had when you were younger may have been due in part to your age, the experience that you had in your life and the current state of society. You may have outgrown these values and belief, and they may no longer apply to you.

Don't let other people's values get in the way of you achieving your goals. We often have adopted values that were essentially given to us by other people. Our parents taught us their values. Some of our values were learned from our grandparents. School teachers gave us some values. We pick up some of our values from church when we were younger. These values sounded good and allowed us to fit into with the people around us but were they and are they still your values as well. It is difficult to work toward achieving values that you do not really believe in. Thus, it is very important to assess who possesses these values that we believe that we hold now.

Next, ask yourself this question: Are you living up to your values and beliefs? If the answer is no, then you need to step back for a second and figure out where the problem lies. Why are you falling short of living by your values and beliefs? The most common answer to this question is that the values and beliefs that you have identified are not truly your values and beliefs; however, they are great ideals that you believe make good values and beliefs.

Are your values in line with your goals? For instance, if you value church, Christianity, and putting out positive messages becoming a rapper is not a goal that fits with these values. When your values and your goals do not align, it is important to determine which one is more important to you and which one needs to fall back so that you can get on your way to achieving your goals or aspire to other goals. You cannot have this conundrum and effectively pursue your goal because there will be a lot of times when your values conflict with what you are asked to or need to do to succeed (unless you want to be a Christian rapper).

Develop A Belief System That is Conducive To you Achieving Your Goals

Restructure your beliefs so that they are in line with your goals. Some of your core beliefs should center around hard work and developing drive to push on and succeed. When your goals and beliefs work together and complement each other, the mental debate that would take place if they were in conflict is eliminated.

It is completely counterproductive to have a belief system that is not in line with the goals that you have set for yourself. Your belief system should push your goals forward.

Identify Your Strengths and Weaknesses

One way to build mental strength is to identify your strengths and weaknesses. Knowing your strengths and weaknesses can help you figure out where you need to improve in order to develop the mental strength that you want.

Ask others for their honest input about what your strengths and weaknesses are. Seek constructive criticism from those around you. Knowing your weaknesses will help you know where to put your focus. Since it is concerning mental strength be sure to ask questions and assess areas which are directly related to mental toughness such as emotional balance, emotional intelligence, mental clarity, drive, focus, and more.

After identifying your weaknesses, write a step by step plan to improve upon each one of these areas so that you can become stronger in these areas. Get other people's opinions as to whether you have any other weaknesses that are not listed so that you can improve upon areas in which other people around you believe that you may be falling short.

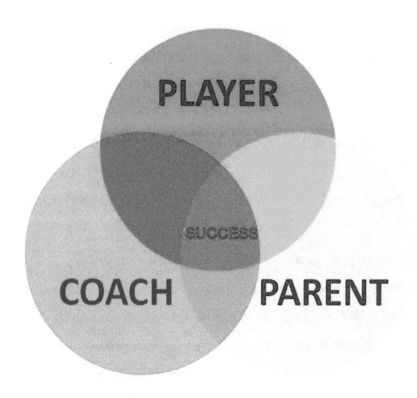

Do Not Allow Your Mental Energy to Be Wasted

Part of developing mental toughness is to develop the ability to focus and eliminate the mental clutter. Learn to differentiate between problems and issues around you that you can do something about and the ones that you cannot. Anything that you cannot do anything about should not be a focus in your mind. You need to accept these things so that you can move on to concentrate on the things that you can control and change.

Also, problems and issues of little significance should not be a focus that weighs on your mind and keeps you from doing other things. Do not concentrate on trivial things that have little to no impact on your life. This will only weigh your mind down, cutting down on the focus and the time that you can give to other things.

Avoid Being a Perfectionist

You need to do things well, and to the best of your ability in life; however, there is a line that when crossed is obsessiveness. Everything does not have to be perfect down to the last detail. Take some time to evaluate how significant the details are about a task or project that you are working on to avoid obsessively trying to be perfect. Perfection is not the key to success, it is the key to obsession, and it should be let go of in order to develop other more important things that are going on around you and in your life.

Actively Eliminate Your Negative Thoughts by Finding Positive Thoughts to Replace Them – Write Down Negative Thoughts When They Creep into Your Mind

When you are trying to accomplish a goal or simply when you are going throughout your day, negative thoughts may creep into your mind. These negative thoughts get to you, the more and more you have them, and they make you less likely to believe that you can achieve and excel at the goals that you have set for yourself.

One active step that you can take to eliminate some of your negative thoughts and their confidence draining effects is to write down your negative thought on a piece of paper. Look at the though and read over it. Is it accurate? Notice what time you experienced the thought and what brought it on. Was it talking to someone that has a negative effect on you? Was it looking at someone who you believe may be more talented than you? It is important for you to notice everything about what brought on the negative thought so that you can understand why the thought crept into your head.

Write all of the negative thoughts that you have in a day down in a journal so that you can see how many negative thoughts creep into your mind during an average day. Do this for a week so that you can notice what days of the week are the best and which are the worst. Where do you tend to be when you have negative thoughts? Maybe consider carrying a mini tape recorder with you so that you can make a note if you have a negative thought at the grocery store.

After writing down all of your negative thoughts and analyzing where they come from and the basis for them, assess what type of an impact of effect the negative thought is having and will have on your performance of your daily tasks and you're achieving the goals that you set out to achieve.

Be sure to notice any patterns that may appear with negative thoughts. Are all of your negative thoughts centered around one goal? If so, this may be a sign that you should let this particular goal go. If something that you want to achieve is always causing you to have negative thoughts, evaluate why these thoughts are raised with this particular goal to see if the goal is one that is worth having.

Are your negative thoughts surrounding a person? Sometimes all of the people in our lives are not good for us and we need to take stock of how a person affects our life before we make the decision on whether or not to keep the person in our life. A toxic friend or a toxic relationship can take a toll on your emotional and mental strength and consume a significant amount of your thoughts. This is a problem that needs to be solved effectively and fast so that you can be more productive. And oftentimes, the solution is cutting the person out of our lives or keeping that person a farther distance away. If this is what it is necessary to do, then make sure that you do this in order to maintain and develop your mental and emotional strength so that you can live a productive fulfilled life.

Come up with positive thoughts to combat some of the negative thoughts that creep into your mind. Think about your strong points and the good things about you and around you that can counteract the negative thought that you are having. Make a list of these positive thoughts and keep them in a journal as well. Try to make sure that your positive thoughts always outweigh your negative ones.

Have a Ceremony to Let Go of The Past

If you often find yourself thinking about past events and occurrences in your life that have had some impact on you whether they were positive or negative, this is counterproductive and not a valuable use of your time or your mind. Still, it is often hard to let go of the past. We often stay stuck in certain moments in our past and relive them in our minds, sometimes even years later. We may dwell on or obsess about past mistakes, wishing that we could go back and change them and thinking about how great our lives would be if we could. But no matter how hard you wish that you could do something to change the past, there is no way that you can, and you have to live for today and tomorrow, not yesterday.

You may have had some negative experiences in the past that you cannot get out of your mind. You may have been mistreated in the past, perhaps you suffered some type of abuse at some point in your life. If you do not want this event to define your entire life, you have to find a way to get it to stop creeping into your mind. Identify the negative thoughts that you have internalized as a result of past events. You may want to write these down as well so that you can take a better look at them. Some of these thoughts may have to do with dealing with certain types or groups of people. Others may have to do with going to different types of events. You need to take the time to think about whether these negative thoughts and feeling that you brought with you are still valid and true today. Sometimes, if we look at our negative experiences again and really think about it, we have moved on in our lives and should be ready and willing to let the past go and start fresh in the present without all of the negatives of the past weighing us down.

If you find that the past is continuously on your mind, you may want to hold a ceremony to release yourself from the past and move into the present. This is true whether the memories in the past that are holding you back are good or bad. If you lost a relative or friend in the past, hold a celebration of life ceremony to remember the person and make a pledge to yourself to not dwell on that event of those memories again. If you were a college football player or cheerleader, have some of your teammates over for a party to reminisce; after the party is over but the memorabilia away and make a vow to move on.

Meditate and reflect on your day at the end of each day.
Each day brings new experiences with it that you can learn from and grow. In addition, there are many repeated experiences that a person has each day that he or she can improve upon. At the end of the day each day, it would be a good idea to take the time to reflect on the day that just passed and think about everything that happened, how you felt, how it affected you, why you believe that certain things occurred, and whether there is anything that you would have done differently.

Try taking about ten minutes at the end of each day to sit quietly in the back of a room, maybe play some meditation music, and strike your favorite yoga pose if you would like and reflect on the day that just occurred so that you can make an assessment of how it went and if there are things that you would do differently or change about your day to make similar days better in the future.

Practice Staying Calm in High-Pressure Situations

Practice has a way of improving the way in which we handle things. That is what it is designed to do, and when it comes to emotional toughness in high-pressure situations, practice may be the best thing that you can do to develop your mental toughness and better handle high-pressure situations.

The main key to succeeding in high-pressure situations is to stay calm and not overreact or become intimidated, but that is often much easier said than done. For example, if you are a musical performer, you can practice your music for hours and hours until you have it perfect when preparing for your first live performance in front of a large crowd. You know that you need to relax and perform the way that you rehearsed, and you are fully prepared; however, this does not guarantee that you are going to execute the performance well when you get in front of that large crowd for the first time. You may execute the performance very poorly once stage fright takes over.

In order for the performer to perform at his or her best when he or she has never done a large live performance before, the performer should practice giving performances in front of smaller crowds and work his or her way up to a larger crowd.

This strategy works well for acclimating one's self to other high-pressure situations as well. Start with lower pressure situations such as the smaller performances and gradually move towards higher and higher-pressure situations as you become more comfortable and acclimated to the pressure situation. This is similar to what organizations such as the military and NASA do with simulators. They simulate actual flight scenarios to train their pilots on how to handle real-world flights.

Additional Ways to Build Mental Toughness

There in addition to the more sophisticated ways to build your mental toughness that are some quick and easy things that you can add to your day. Here are some other interesting ways that many people have found to have an actual effect on building their mental toughness.

Cold Showers

One such way that has worked for a number of people that you may not have thought of or come across in other places is to take cold showers. Taking cold showers can help you clear your mind and get your blood flowing and your adrenaline pumping. This can help to elevate your level of concentration and focus so that you can get on your way to achieving a goal that you set that day or having an outstanding performance.

Disconnect Yourself from Social Media

Social media is a huge phenomenon that has turned into a staple of our current culture and is here to stay. The problem with social media, however, is that it is full of tweets, blurbs, Snapchats, Instagram photos with a one-liner underneath and more tic-tacky stuff that can occupy a person's entire day with no educational or informative information being supplied. This makes it an interesting distraction; however, not something that you should be constantly utilizing throughout your day.

Constantly taking breaks to check social media or even waiting for your breaks to check social media is a distraction from what you should be doing and a break in your concentration. Unless you are actually making a significant amount of money from one of the social media channels, at which point you can consider the utilization of social media working, this is not a productive use of your time, and significant limits should be placed on your use of social media so that you can fill your mind with productive, informative, educational or insightful things.

Always Be Reading A Self-Help Book on A Subject Area in Which You Can Improve

Another way to increase your mental toughness is to expand your mind and learn new things that can improve your mental toughness, your emotional stability, your emotional intelligence and more. There are thousands of books out there on how you can improve, take control of, and master just about anything in your life. You should always be reading one of them in order to gain the information that is contained on the pages and help yourself learn how to grow and improve in this area. This is a great way to spend your free time, your lunch break, your daily commute on the subway and more. You can learn how to make friends and influence people, learn about mastery, learn the 48 laws of power, learn how to control your emotions, learn how to budget better, learn how to have more self-confidence and more by reading a book in that subject area for a few minutes a day. Constantly learning and expanding your mind is a trait of people who possess and exhibit mental strength.

Chapter 2: Fear and Stress

Unfortunately, both fear and stress are a part of daily life. Fear is an emotion that is characterized by a feeling of intense distress to a situation which is perceived to be threatening. Stress is a biological response to an environmental condition, whether it be a threat or a physical or psychological barrier. In essence, stress is the perception that a high-pressure situation is occurring and a person's internal response to the pressure.

Both fear and stress and have a negative impact on your mental state and emotions. They can be draining on a person's energy level and ability to concentrate. These emotions can clog a person's mind if they get out of control and become the main factor that people focus on.

How Fear Affects Mental Toughness

Fear affects the mind and the emotions in a way that may be hard for some people to control or even predict. The way that you react to fear often depends on the fear stimuli, the perceived intensity of the threat and how well you react to high-pressure situations in general. Other values such as self-preservation versus caring for others also come into play.

Fear diminishes some of the characteristics of mental toughness that are part of the unbeatable mind. If these elements of mental toughness are not fully developed in a person or the person is not able to adequately cope with the feeling of fear, some of the element of mental toughness that a person would generally count on to pull him or her out of a tough situation may not be able to be utilized at optimal levels.

Fears effects on the elements of the Unbeatable Mind and Mental Toughness
Fear can actually affect the first trait of the unbeatable mind, mental capacity if the fear is strong enough or a person is unable to handle and cope with fear properly. People who experience strong fear are often known to have breakdowns.

Even though fear diminishes the characteristics of mental strength if you do not know how to react to it properly, developing your mental toughness can actually help a person cope with and react to fear better. Mental toughness can help you react in a more productive manner to fear. The reason that there is a productive way in which people can react to fear has to do with the fact that fear is not an entirely negative emotion even though many people may initially categorize it as such. Fear is actually necessary for survival in dangerous situations. The fear emotion warns a person that there is a great danger ahead.

Although fear is not entirely a negative emotion, as it does serve to warn you of danger, it is an emotion that can stop you from pursuing and achieving your goals. Fear can keep you from doing the things that you want to do in life. Thus, it is crucial for you to be able to handle fear properly in order to get the things done that you would like to get done in your life or participate in the activities in which you would like to participate. For instance, you may want to participate in a sport like football; however, you have a significant fear of being injured. If you focus on your fear and do not handle it properly, you may choose not to play football, and you will miss out on participating in something that you really wanted to do.

Stress Causes:	Mental Toughness Causes:
	With practice immersing one's self into a high-pressure situation, a person can stay calm under pressure.
A feeling of being overwhelmed.	Time management skills.

How Stress Affects Mental Toughness

There are some causes of stress that are common to everyone according to polls and studies. These common causes of stress include job and workplace stress, financial stress, stress over personal relationships, stress over daily hassles, stress from having too many things to do and too little time, and stress over family and children. Stress is a part of daily life that is unavoidable. However, we all know that stress has a very negative effect on the body. It is an emotion that can heighten performances in some and lead to an emotional breakdown in other people.

Unlike fear which tends to be caused by something that scares a person in some way, stress is caused by being worried about something, whether it be something that scares you or not. There are some things that traditionally tend to cause a person to feel stressed. One of the primary causes of stress is being under a lot of pressure.

A significant amount of pressure can cause a person to feel a great deal of stress. This pressure may be caused by having a lot of things to do at work, too many family obligations, having to perform in a sporting event, having too much to do and feeling that you do not have a lot of time to get it all done and more. When you are under a significant amount of pressure and thus stressed out, your mind is filled with thoughts of whatever is stressing you out making it hard to concentrate and think as clearly as you would have if you were more relaxed. This affects the mental toughness or strength that you currently possess because you may see that the positive traits of mental strength diminish in these situations if you have not trained yourself to handle stress.

7 MENTAL SKILLS EVERY GYMNAST NEEDS
PLUS
7 TECHNIQUES YOU SHOULD BE USING

Something else that may trigger stress and thus affect mental strength is emotional things. Things which are emotional include relationships with spouses, friends, family, and others around you, the inability to find a job, the need for more money and wondering where and how you are going to get it and more. Although some of these stressors are mental as well, they tend to be very emotional. If you have not developed your emotional intelligence, you may become overrun by your emotions, thus losing mental strength. We have all seen this happen to someone; a person seems to have it all together, seems to be very smart, has a good job, and is highly functional until he or she is going through a breakup or a divorce and that person seems to start to unravel. If you are not equipped with the emotional intelligence and mental toughness to handle emotionally stressing situations, you may become too stressed out to function at your normal level.

Another common cause of stress is facing significant changes in your life. This may start to seem overwhelming to you and cause you to fail to react in your normal way, fail to think things through in a logical manner, or otherwise fail to do everything that you need to do for these changes to go smoothly. This can cause you to question whether or not you are mentally fit to go through these changes. You may start to believe, especially at times when things start to seem more difficult, that you were only mentally strong enough for the way your life was before the changes and even start to resist change or want things to change back to the way that they were. If you have trained yourself to have the mental strength to cope with this type of situation, it will go more smoothly, and you may even enjoy the significant changes that come in your life.

Feeling a lack of control over the things that take place around you, or your life, in general, can cause you to feel significantly stressed out. You may believe that you do not know what to expect in life and that nothing you do seems to have a significant impact on the way that things turn out for you. All of the preparation and the planning that you do seems to be for nothing. This type of stress can diminish your resolve, affect your ability to set goals, your willpower and more due to the fact that you may fail to see the point of doing these things.

There are certain times in your life when things are uncertain. You do not know what is going to happen. You may be worried about the future or even what is going to take place in the present. These are the times when stress tends to form and build up. This undoubtedly affects how you are able to function and your thought processes.

The problem with stress is that it does not just include the mental emotion of feeling tense or anxious or the inability to concentrate as well as you should. Many people have a strong physical reaction to stress, and you could be one of them. Stress causes the human body to experience a number of negative health consequences. Some of these reactions are minor, and some are more severe. If a person is under stress for a significant period of time and does not take the time to address the issue properly, this can take a major toll on the person's health.

Some significant changes can occur in your body due to high-stress levels and some significant health problems that can result. This is the primary reason that it is important to manage stress properly. Some of the most common effect that stress has on your body include headaches, fatigue, problems falling asleep and staying asleep, muscle pain and tense muscles, nausea. Mentally stress can cause an inability to focus, lack of motivation, a feeling of being overwhelmed, depression, irritability restlessness and more. The most severe effects of unregulated stress over a long period of time are high blood pressure, obesity heart disease, and diabetes. Stress can also lead to some negative coping behaviors which compound the health problems that it can cause. Some of the negative coping strategies that stress produces include the use of alcohol and tobacco as well as the use and abuse of prescription and illegal drugs. It can also lead to overeating as a person tries to consume comfort food and may neglect to eat a proper diet. Withdrawn from social interaction is another result of being under too much pressure and stress.

You have probably heard of a type A personality; this is the type of personality that business executives and the like tend to have. They are under stress a lot and tend to develop health problems as a result if they do not find proper outlets to cope with stress.

Use Mental Toughness to Deal with Fear and Stress

Yes, you can use mental toughness to better deal with fear and stress. Mental toughness addresses some of the underlying causes of both fear and stress. Addressing the underlying issues is one of the primary ways that you want to handle these two emotions so that you can mitigate them.

Mental toughness and developing your mental strength can help a person react to fear in a more positive manner that makes the experience of fearless detrimental to the person and even allows the person to think strategically in order to get through the fear-filled situation. Fear is a state of mind that can be altered. It is not just your reaction to fear but also whether and how much fear you feel in all a part of your mind and your emotions.

Moreover, both the amount of stress that you feel and the way that you handle the stress that you do feel can be altered with mental toughness training. Training your mind to help you stay calm in high-pressure situations and taking steps to become more responsible can affect how much stress you feel. The way that you handle stress can be altered by the plan that you develop to handle the underlying situation as well as the calming techniques that you use.

Perception

Developing your mental toughness can help you deal with stress because the amount of stress that you feel in a situation often depends on certain variables. One of these variables is the way that you perceive the situation that is the central cause of the stress or from which the stressor is arising. The way that you perceive a situation may have to do with past experiences. Past experiences can include your own past experiences with a given situation as well as past experiences watching a parent, older sibling, family member, or someone else deals with the same situation.

Another factor that ways into how you perceive a situation is your self-esteem. A person with lower self-esteem may become more stressed out when thinking about relocating to a new area or getting a new job because he or she may wonder how he is going to meet and fit in with new people. Your level of self-esteem can be elevated with emotional intelligence training, a subject which is discussed in the last chapter of this book.

Yet, another factor that goes into how you perceive a situation is how you tend to perceive things in general. Do you tend to perceive things more positively or negatively? Are you a positive or a negative person? If you typically have a lot of negative thoughts that you tend to leave unchecked, this could have a significant impact on the way you perceive the situations that arise and how stressed out you become as a result of these situations. One of the common traits that people with mental toughness display is a propensity to think positively and to see the upside about a given situation. Furthermore, as discussed in the chapter concerning Ways to Develop Mental Strength, you should identify your negative thoughts, address why you have formed those thoughts and whether they are accurate or inaccurate, and actively combat these thoughts with more positive thoughts.

Perspective

Perspective is pretty close to perception, but it differs slightly. Perspective has to do with the angle at which you are looking at things. You have surely heard the phrase "try to keep things in perspective." This means that the lens through which you look at an event or situation should be in focus so that it does not magnify it to the point that it is no longer in perspective. You need to be able to judge things that occur for the significance that they actually have. You need to not place too much importance on things that do not have an equal amount of significance. Developing mental toughness can help you put things into perspective and keep them in perspective. Putting things in the proper perspective comes from mental competency as well as emotional intelligence and emotional balance.

Your Experience with The Pressure Situation

Your own experience with a particular pressure situation has a significant impact on the amount of stress and fear that you experience when facing that situation. Let's say, for instance, you are a college basketball player playing in a game, and you have been fouled. The stands are full, and the game is televised. If this is your first game, you may experience a sudden pang of fear when thinking about how you are going to execute the foul shot and you may have been stressed out about the game all week. However, if you are into your junior year and you play regularly, the fear that you used to feel during your freshman season may have subsided and the amount of stress that the impending game caused you all week may be virtually non-existent.

One key way to develop mental toughness when handling a stressful situation such as the one described above is to immerse yourself in a stressful situation starting with situations that are a lower level of stress and increase the pressure until you get to the higher level of pressure which is the game. This will help you to curb your fear, and the amount of stress that this situation causes you to experience will be less than it would if you had not taken this step. In addition, repeated practicing is the key to being comfortable in a given situation. This applies not only to sports but to most other areas of life as well.

Another example of how your personal experiences affect how much stress you feel in a given situation and how much fear it brings on is that of the end of a relationship. If you have been in relationships before and they always ended with a breakup, some of the things that lead to the break up may still be in the back of your mind as well as the feelings of loss that you felt from the break up itself. You may bring these feelings and experiences into a new relationship, and this may affect what you feel, thus bringing pressure and stress in the new relationship. You may even fear breaking up with may cause you to be more passive and less self-assured. This may be a change from the behavior that you displayed in your previous relationships in which you may have displayed more confidence and were less timid. You may have tried to force things to fit less and felt more secure about the relationship as a whole. Because your previous experiences with relationships were negative in that they always ended with breakups, you needed to have dealt with your emotions as a result of these experiences properly including honing your emotional intelligence skills to be more in tune with your partner. This is a topic that is cover in more detail in the last chapter of this book.

Other Pressures

The amount of stress that you feel over a given situation is also controlled by the amount of stress that you are under in general. If you have a lot of responsibilities and you are having a difficult time fitting them all in and managing your time, this can cause you to feel a great deal of stress and even fear. Thus, your perception of a specific situation does not have to be the things upon which the stress is based, and which triggers the feeling of fear. Every situation that you are dealing with right then can compound themselves into a giant stressful situation if you do not take the effective steps in trying to handle each situation as it arises. This is where the discipline and willpower that is developed when practicing and developing mental toughness come in.

Addressing issues in the appropriate amount of time can keep things from spiraling out of control and minimize that amount that you have on your plate at one time. The importance of this cannot be underestimated because you may look back at the situation later and realize that none of the individual issues would have caused so much stress and fear if they had been addressed and handled alone but because they were not, these issues snowballed into what seemed like an impending catastrophe which can cause great fear and stress that should have been avoided with proper planning.

Your Emotional Stability

Your emotional stability has a great deal to do with how much stress you experience. People who are overly emotional or who have less control over their emotions may find themselves experiencing a great deal of stress whereas people who have more control over their emotions may find the situations that the other person found stressful to be moderately easy situations to handle.

If you've experienced a similar situation in the past and your emotions are still raw, or you've experienced a significant amount of negative emotion about that situation in the past, this can have a significant effect on the amount of stress that experience due to that situation. In fact, if your emotions alone can have a huge impact on your perception of whether or not something is a stressful situation or one that evolves fear. Thus, emotional intelligence training is very significant in this type of situation. You need to get in touch with your own emotions as well as learn to assess and identify the triggers for these emotions so that you know where they are coming from and where they originate. Making strides in your level of emotional stability will allow you to experience less stress and fear in many situations as well as handle these emotions better.

Your Values

Your values also play a key role in how much stress you will experience in a given situation, the solutions that you come up with to handle it and the amount of fear that both the problem and the solution cause. This is because your values decide what is important to you and it is what you deem to be important that determines whether you fear losing it or stress out about it. For example, a law school student who places high importance on getting good grades on his exams so that he can get a job at a top-notch law firm would be stressed out if he did not have time to study. A student in the same class that is more interested in doing community service work and does not care about grades, only passing would stress out a lot less over the same situation. Worrying about grades is only in line with the first student's values and not the values of the second student. Thus, the same situation cannot evoke the same amount of stress in both students.

Because values are so central to the amount of stress that you experience, you should examine your values and alter them in a way that will allow you to feel less stress and handle things properly. If you value money and you are constantly stressing out over when you will have money and whether or not you will have enough money, maybe you should examine whether money should be one of your values. Constantly stressing out about money suggests that your aspirations for money are not leading to happiness; instead, your aspiration for money is leading to unhappiness. Try lowering money a little on your value list and find solutions to make ends meet with the amount of money that you already have. You may want to try downsizing or budgeting better to satisfy your money needs instead of trying to obtain more money.

This is why it is important to set relevant goals (remember SMART goals), to ensure that your goals are relevant to your present and your future. Likewise, your goals should be attainable. You should not go around chasing goals and dreams that you cannot seem to ever catch; especially if there is a good chance that you never will. It is also important to assess your values to ensure that they truly are and should be the things that you value. In addition, the use of mentally strong traits such as willpower can help you take steps to stick to goals that are in line with the values that really matter to you.

Your Support System

Your personal support system is critical to the amount of stress and fear that you feel in a given situation. Thus, this is one of the most significant factors in determining how much stress and fear you experience. A person with a strong support system may feel little to no stress in situations in which a person with a weak support system would get stressed out. One of the primary examples of this is when a person is stressing out about money. A person with a significant support system which includes parents, siblings, and friends from whom the person can borrow money would not stress out nearly as much as a person who has to try to make ends meet on his or her own. The first person may try to0 keep his or her finances in order and to make sure he always has the money for rent and the car note; however, the second person must make sure that he or she succeeds in always having the money for rent and the car note. There is much less room for error and a potential for a far more stressful situation to form with the second person that there is with the first person due to the inadequate support system that the second person has.

Another example of how your support system factors in is with the above example of a breakup. A person with a strong support system may bounce back more quickly due to friends and relatives being supportive of the person and spending time with him or her. The amount of loss is minimized in this instance because there was a strong enough support system that the person does not feel a significant void in his or her life. This can also result in the person being less fearful of a breakup. People with an adequate support system may be more likely to let a relationship go if it is not working out and move on.

Building a strong support system is part of developing your mental strength. This is because the people that you have around you impact your thoughts, attitudes, beliefs, and values, People who exhibit mental toughness often choose to be around other people who have this type of mental training. They are positive people who tend not to bring them down or hold them back in life because part of developing mental strength is recognizing the type of people that do hold you back. Use emotional intelligence skills to assess the people around you and make sure that they are the type of people that you should be around. Eliminating people from your life is tough; however, it is often necessary to get rid of negative vibes and influences in your life.

Your Amount of Discipline

There are some positive coping strategies for dealing with stress, but they take discipline. Thus, you must develop this mental strength skill in order to handle stress properly. One of these positive coping strategies to reduce stress properly is through regular exercise. Exercise is a healthy way to release some stress and anger while burning calories and keeping in shape. Another positive technique to release stress positively is to make sure that you have time for the things that you enjoy such as hobbies and past times away from work and taking care of responsibilities. This requires proper time management. Spending time with friends and family is yet another way to relieve stress healthily. Relaxation techniques can also help reduce the amount of stress that you are feeling, as well as your level of irritability while keeping your blood pressure and heart rate normal. Some relaxation techniques include yoga, deep breathing, meditation, massages, and tai chi.

Chapter 6: Setting Goals

Goal setting is an important component of accomplishing the things that you want to accomplish in life. To be productive and accomplish goals you must first clearly identify the goal that you would like to accomplish. It is important for these goals to be as clearly defined as possible and not vague or ambiguous. Clearly defining the goal helps to put you in the mindset to accomplish this goal.

Mental toughness directly applies to goal setting. As stated earlier, people with significant mental strength set goals, often in a series, starting with the easiest and quickest goal to accomplish and moving on to more and more complex goals.

Key elements to goal setting.

1) **Make sure that the goals that you set are goals that you are motivated to achieve.**

One of the best ways to accomplish goals is to set goals that you really want to accomplish. Goals that you are excited about and look forward to starting and completing are goals that you are more likely to stick to and accomplish.

This may seem easier said than done with some goals because often you must set goals for completing homework, school work, or work which may not truly excite you. However, it is still important to find and identify a motivating force behind the goal so that you will strive to achieve it. The motivating force could be getting a weekend off to do something that you really love or getting the raise that you wanted. Either way, both the goal and the motivation behind the goal should be very clear and specific in order to encourage yourself to complete the goal.

2) Write your goal down and inform people about it.
After you have clearly identified your goals and the
motivation behind clearly, you need to neatly write them
down or print them out and post them on the wall. You need
your goals to be displayed concretely so that you cannot brush
them under the rug and forget about them.

Furthermore, you should let your friends and family know
what your goals are so that they are now 'publicized' in your
world. This will help you stick to your goals because telling
people about them makes them more real. After you have told
the people around you about your goals, it becomes harder to
put them off or deviate from them due to lack of willpower, a
belief that the goals that you have set are not urgent or other
reasons. Friends and family can encourage you to stick to your
goals. They are a great source of emotional support that will
aid you when you want to achieve something. They can often
help you out on the way to achieving your goals and remind
you of what they are.

Another way that friends, family, and the people around you encourage you to stick to your goals is that once they are announced, there is a sort of shame in going back on your word. Not sticking to your goals after telling people about them may make you seem flaky and cause people not to take you as seriously in other aspects of your life. It will seem as though you cannot keep your word, even if it is only to yourself. Part of the reason that telling people about your goals is included is because once you tell people that you are going to do something, it is best that you actually stick to it and do it.

3) Set SMART goals.

S (Specific)	Goals need to be as specific as possible.
M (Measurable)	Goals need to be measurable.
A (Attainable)	Goals need to be attainable by *you*.
R (Relevant)	Goals need to be relevant to you.
T (Time-Bound)	Goals need to have specific time constraints set on them.

All of the MBA programs and many articles about goal setting today are talking about setting SMART goals. SMART is an acronym which makes all of the parts that the goal must include easier to remember. SMART stands for S) Specific Goals, M) Measurable Goals, A) Attainable Goals, R) Relevant Goals, and T) Time-Bound Goals.

S) Specific Goals

According to the SMART goals philosophy and as mentioned above, the goals that you set should be as specific as possible. Make sure that the goals that you set are as specific as possible. This means that you should not leave any significant questions concerning exactly what your goal is open for debate, discussion or confusion. It is very important that you fully flesh out your goals so that you can understand what they are and what you need to do to achieve them.

The main problem with not specifically detailing your goal is that you may not be exactly sure of what you want to do. This uncertainty lends itself more to being termed a wish than a goal because it is not specific enough to be noted as a goal.

Making your goals as specific as possible allows you to think about in advance whether or not this was the true end goal. This is very important because oftentimes the answer is no, and the goal needs to be changed slightly or maybe even significantly for you to ultimately get what you what after you achieve your goal. I'm am sure you have heard the saying "Be careful what you wish for, you just might get it," detailing your specific goal can lessen the changes that what you wished for wasn't really what you wanted.

M) Measurable Goals

The goals that you set should be measurable, meaning that there is a specific amount, date, or length of time in which the goal needs to be accomplished. Do not leave the goal vague as to amounts and things of that nature because these values may soon start to decrease. If you first wanted to save up $5000, and you don't write down the exact amount of money that you wanted to save, this value may soon decrease to $3000 when you get tired of working and it starts to take you a little longer than you thought that it would and not be as easy as you thought that it would be to save up the money. This is where mental toughness comes into play. If you set a specific and measurable goal, you can use some of the tips included in this book to

A) Attainable Goals

It is important for the goals that you set to be attainable *by you*. Although you want to strive to achieve as much as you can, it does you very little good to set goals which are impossible to achieve. This is a waste of time and will only lead to frustration. Instead, when identifying the goal with specificity, make sure that all of the specific parts of the goal are attainable. You need to be qualified to achieve each part of the goal.

Everybody wants to accomplish such a great feat in life or to be notable and standout in some way. You can stand out more by accomplishing what you set out to accomplish that by setting a goal that was so out of reach that you never can achieve it. Goals should not be so easy and simple that you don't have to work for them or that you should have expected to achieve them rather easily; however, they should not be entirely too difficult to achieve either.

R) Relevant Goals

All of your goals should apply to things that you actually want to accomplish and that benefit you. At first, you may assume that since you are the one who is setting the goal, this would automatically be true; however, it is not a given. This is because people often get their ideas from somewhere or someone else. For instance, when setting goals for your New Year's resolutions, many people may select some common and popular resolutions that seem like positive things to aim for, however, these resolutions may not have been something that the person actually interested in, *they only thought that they were.* Common goals which are positive in nature and seem like goals for which you should aspire to, are not the same as goals that you actually do aspire to.

Your goals should be relevant to you at the time and place you are now in your life and taking into account where you would like to be in the future. One mistake that people make when they fail to reexamine their goals every so often is that their goals may be relevant to them; however, they apply to how the person was in the past. Thus, goals need to be relevant to both *you* and *now.*

T) Time-Bound Goals

Goals should be time-bound. The best way to encourage yourself to start on a goal is to set a deadline. This deadline needs to be concrete in order to encourage you to keep moving on the way to your goal. Set a deadline that is realistic but does show some sense of urgency.

Goals with no time limit are goals that you may take forever to complete. This is because there is no sense of urgency and you can always justify putting them off while telling yourself that you are sticking to your goals and that you are focused and determined to succeed and achieve them. This is because it is difficult to not still be on course to achieve a goal that you have an infinite amount of time to fulfill. You can always keep telling yourself that you will start on the goal tomorrow.

Move goals into action with an action plan.

Devising an action plan for your goals is the best way to move them from simple aspirations to things that you are actively trying to accomplish. After identifying the goal with specificity, you will need to identify each step along the way to achieving your goal. You may want to group the steps into subheading categories but be sure to list every single thing that you need to do to get to your goal. When you break the end goal into smaller steps, each small step is easier to achieve and does not take as much time, energy, and determination as the larger goal itself; thus, these smaller steps are easier to handle and make the larger goals seem less intimidating and more doable.

5. Incorporate your goals into your daily routine.

Identify a part of your goal that you can do everyday so that each day you are at least taking one small step toward your goal every day. This is a great way to not only break your goal up into small and accomplishable parts; it is a way to make your goal a part of your daily routine. It is much harder to put the goal off or forget about it if it is part of your every day routine. Furthermore, it will seem as if it takes less willpower to get to your goal.

Goals and mental toughness

Developing some of the common traits of mental strength can help you set and achieve your goals. The first trait of mentally strong people that will help you along the way to achieving your goals is mental competency. Ensuring that you are mentally competent can make sure that your goals are realistic and help you to put the importance of these goals into perspective.

Other traits such as resilience, willpower, emotional intelligence, having a winner's mind, possessing the ability to focus, surrounding yourself with mentally strong people, and avoiding bucking the system too often all work together to help a person achieve his or her goals. All of these characteristics are necessary to possess and cultivate if you want to attain higher and higher levels of achievement.

Chapter 3: Emotional Intelligence

What Is Emotional Intelligence?

Emotional intelligence is the ability to recognize and understand your own emotions as well as the emotions of others. It has a variety of different definitions with no one definition being superior to the others. Some texts define emotional intelligence as having four fundamental parts which include: managing emotions, perceiving emotions, understanding emotions, and using emotions. Other texts consider emotional intelligence to be self-awareness, social awareness, relationship management, self-management, and emotional intelligence. Still more consider emotional intelligence to be composed of five parts; these five parts are social skills, self-awareness, self-regulation, motivation, and empathy. One thing that is agreed upon is that emotional intelligence consists of being both aware of your own self and your emotions as well as being conscious of the people around you and their emotions.

Emotional intelligence gives you the ability to differentiate between different emotions that you may experience and identify and label each one correctly. This skill is a very important skill for people to possess because understanding your own emotions and being able to differentiate between them gives you the opportunity to control your emotions and take steps to adjust them. For instance, if you notice that a given thing makes you depressed, you can take steps to counter that in advance to avoid or minimize this emotional response.

Understanding and being able to differentiate between the emotions, responses, and behaviors of others allows you to interact better with other people. This is very important because a great deal of our lives has to do with interaction with other people. You can benefit from this in almost every facet of your life. A salesman can understand body language, and facial expressions, and understands which statements a person may take offense.

The Ability to Listen to Your Emotions

Emotional intelligence is also the ability to listen to and adjust your thinking and behavior based on the information that your emotions are giving you.

For it to be a good idea, however, for you to listen to your emotions and be guided by them, you need to have the ability to keep your emotions in balance.

Your emotions need to be under control before it is okay to listen to them. It would not be wise for an overly emotional person to listen to and be guided by his or her emotions. Thus, you must be able first to identify your emotions, and then understand where your emotions are coming from and what triggers them. Is it an event from the past? Is it negative thoughts about your worthiness? Is it an overly inflated ego? It is important to understand whether your emotions are coming from the event or person that you are dealing with or something else before you judge your reaction.

Your emotions need to provide you with accurate information in order for you to be able to use them in a manner that is beneficial to you. Thus, you need to be in tune with your emotions and tune them up from time to time so that the information that they are presenting to you is useful and accurate and thus a good guide for your behavior.

Why Do You Need Emotional Intelligence?

Everyone *needs* to have emotional intelligence, and it can definitely make your life easier if you have a great deal of emotional intelligence. The ability to understand the way that others are thinking, feeling and may react as well as being in touch with your own emotions that are formed for the situations that are in can help you navigate through situations in daily life far more effectively and with greater ease than you would if you lacked this skill.

It is important for a person to understand how his or her emotions connect to his or her behavior. Emotions have a significant effect on how a person perceives things, and in turn how he or she reacts to it. If you do not understand and are not in control of your emotions, you may not understand the reason for your reaction. Many people never even bother to think about why they react a certain way to certain things. Your behavior directly relates to your reaction to certain stimuli.

Furthermore, the way in which other people react and behave toward you is directly correlated to the emotions that they feel when they are around you as well. So, it is best to be in tune to the so that you can do well. In fact, people with a high degree of emotional intelligence often manipulate other people's emotions to tilt situations in their favor.

When Do You Need Emotional Intelligence?

There are a significant number of situations in life when you need to have emotional intelligence so it would be wise to think that it is always good to have and utilize emotional intelligence. In fact, it can be argued that the only time that you do not need to have emotional intelligence is when you are sleeping...alone. This is because life is filled with interactions between other people and these interactions often involve emotions.

In Relationships

One of the most obvious times in which you can benefit from having emotional intelligence is in your personal relationships. Relationships are often filled with and even based on emotions.

Knowing when your spouse or significant other is happy, upset, or annoyed can help your relationship run a lot smoother, so does knowing the right thing to say and when to say it. Awkward people, people without adequate people skills often have a difficult time meeting people and thus forming relationships. If you have no clue what to say to the opposite sex, when or what they may find offensive, you may have a difficult time finding a mate, most cases are not this extreme, and most people do have some emotional intelligence; however, improving your emotional intelligence can help you to enjoy your relationships more, form more relationships and closer bonds with other people, feel less intimidated in social situations and network better with others.

At Work

Although it may not seem as though emotional intelligence comes into play as much at work, if there are other people around you at work, and these people are likely to experience emotions, then emotional intelligence can be a great asset to you in the workplace. In fact, emotional intelligence can help your workday go more smoothly, help you to get along with your coworkers better, get the people around you to look more favorably upon your ability to do your work and even get you a raise or a promotion that you have wanted for a long time.

The first time you use emotional intelligence at work is at the job interview itself. Since the interviewer may be seeing a number of different candidates, you do not only want to make sure that you impress him or her with your credentials and impressive resume, you also want to make sure that you do not rub the person the wrong way. Yes, catering to your interviewer's emotions is important if you want to land that job.

You know you need to be able to read signals and take hints in order to secure the position. But what does taking hints involve? Taking hints and reading signals involves identifying the emotions of the interviewer and acting according to what is pleasing to him or her. Or, it may mean realizing that this is not a person that you want to work with and that you need to look for another job. Either way, it is important for you to be in tune with the thoughts and feelings of the interviewer so that you can perform well or make a judgement call as to whether this is an environment that you can work in.

Emotional Intelligence versus Intellectual Intelligence

When looking at the benefits of having emotional intelligence, one has to wonder which one is better to possess, emotional intelligence or intellectual intelligence. Intellectual intelligence is a test of someone's academic intelligence and is often measured by standardized tests. Intellectual intelligence gauges your ability to learn and understand information that is being presented to you. In addition, it is representative of your logical reasoning ability, reading comprehension skills and often reading and math skills as well. This type of intelligence is very beneficial to have in the workplace and is often an indicator of who will perform well at the tasks assigned and shine at his or her job.

How to Gain Emotional Intelligence

Emotional intelligence is important to have since so much of life is spent dealing with other people, and you also need to understand your own emotions in order to be successful and enjo0y your life. Some people may be blessed with emotional intelligence already, and these people may know who they are. They are the ones who are always making friends and have an easy time with people. Even still, they may not have developed their emotional intelligence skills in all situations and environments. A person can have a high level of emotional intelligence with their friends but a very low level of emotional intelligence at work. This can come from feeling connected to friends and taking the time to listen and emphasize while, at the same time, feeling disconnected at work and not making the same effort to understand the emotions of others and interact with them well. This type of person can benefit from learning how to gain emotional intelligence as it applies to different situations.

Other people may have a more difficult time around people and fail to make friends easily. They may also have trouble relating to people at work. They may even experience some anxiety when they are in situations where they are meeting people for the first time. If you are one of these people, you probably already believe that you need some extra help when dealing with other people and trying to understand how to better interact with them. You simply may not have been aware that increasing your emotional intelligence can help you do this.

Here are some ways that you can improve upon your emotional intelligence:

1) Get in touch with your own emotions by taking time to reflect on them.

Emotional intelligence involves not only understanding the emotions of others; it also involves getting in touch with your own emotions as well. This is important when interacting with others because the way people think, feel and act towards you may be significant in the way you interact with them. It is also significant to how you perceive the experience no matter how it goes.

Because it is so important to understand your emotions in different situations, you need to get in touch with your emotions and the best way to do this is by taking the time to think about them actively. Reflect on your emotions through the day at the end of the day. Jot down the emotions that you experienced in different situations, how you felt, whether or not you enjoyed it. Did something make you nervous? Did you experience fear?

Understanding what emotions you experience in different situations can allow you to gain better control over your emotions. This is especially true if you are a person who experiences anger issues. Determining exactly what type of events may trigger anger in you will help you to control it better.

2) Solicit the opinions of others.

When assessing emotions and trying to gain a great understanding of how yourself and others think and feel, it is important to get other people's opinions. This is because another person may view a situation differently than you do and may experience different emotions in the same situation. Another person may even offer you a different way for you to look at a situation that is troubling you or you have not figured out how to handle on your own.

Ask as many questions as you can about different situations and scenarios that you face and interactions that you have so that you can gain the most accurate insight into how the other people involved and even the people watching think and feel about the situation.

3) Stop and think before doing some things or having some interactions

Normally, we go through our day doing the things we need to do and interacting with the people that we need to interact with without thinking about it first. Take a moment to stop and think about some of these things before you do them and some interactions before you have them. As yourself what do you expect to feel about doing this? How would you feel if you did not do it today? How do you think that this interaction is going to go? Do you think that you will enjoy the interaction? Are you dreading it?

After taking the time to stop and think and asking yourself some of the questions listed above, you may want to jot the answers down on a piece of paper and slip it in your pocket.

After the event or interaction takes place, think about whether it went the way you expected and whether it went differently because you stopped and thought about it. Answering the first question will help you to understand how closely your expectations about the event or interaction coincided with the actual occurrence. After doing this a few times you may be able to see where your perception is off and start bringing your expectations beforehand and the actual occurrence closer to matching. Answering the second question, 'Do you believe that the event or interaction went the same way or that it went different from what it would have if you had not stopped and thought about the situation first?' can help you understand whether you need to take the time out to think about your actions, thoughts, and interactions before you have the to make sure that you are in control of your emotion and react the best way that you possibly can to the situation.

4) Observe and study the emotions and interactions of others.

To learn more about how other people experience emotions and how they think and react to things, it is a good idea to simply watch them for a while so that you can see for yourself how they experience certain situations.

Maybe go to a local park or a shopping mall, sit on the bench and simply watch people when they walk by. How do people seem to treat each other? Are people who do not know each other polite to each other?

Jot down so notes about some of the things that you see. Especially note the reactions that you did not expect and maybe hypothesize as to why your opinion of what the reaction would be was wrong.

5) Practice putting yourself in situations which may help to improve your interactions with others and your ability to understand their emotions.

If you are uncomfortable meeting people, you should not try to avoid such situations. On the contrary, you should go to as many of these types of events and place yourself in as many of these situations as possible until you get better at it. (Important Note: If you really need practice in this area, it may be best to start off in some places where you do not have to worry about seeing the people again. Try and out of state conference for a hobby or interest of yours and see how you do at mixing and mingling. Or try going to a nightclub or bar in a neighboring city, mingling and asking someone to dance with you. You can even stay at a hotel overnight and think about your experience.

The more experience you gain in certain situations, the better you will become at understanding them and handling them with poise ease and grace. So, go out there and practice interacting and take notes to see how this improves your level of emotional intelligence. Practicing certain situations which you find socially challenging is also part of developing mental toughness, the ability to endure and succeed in the given situation through practice and perseverance. And take notes!

6) Learn to handle criticism well and even learn from it. Sometimes, as you go throughout your day something that you have done or said may receive some criticism from someone else. Do take this personally. On the contrary, try to learn to handle criticism, so long as it is not too harsh, in a constructive manner. Ask the person who gives the criticism of what he or she saw wrong with the situation that led up to the criticism. If there really is a flaw of some sort, this gives you the opportunity to fix it. And even if you do not agree with the criticism, you get to hear the other person's thoughts and feelings on the matter which leads to an improvement in your level of emotional intelligence.

The Negative Effects of Not Having Emotional Intelligence
There are a number of negative effects of not having emotional intelligence. In fact, if you lack emotional intelligence, you are probably experiencing the negative effects and may even know what they are.

People who do not have emotional intelligence struggle when dealing with other people, some may not even realize it. Emotional intelligence is often referred to as people skills. People with poor people skills tend to misread situations and may say things that are inappropriate or even offensive due to the fact that they have a lowered ability to read other people.

As stated earlier in this book, empathy, or the ability to empathize with others is a trait that a person needs in order to have a higher level of emotional intelligence and form significant connections to others. Without the ability to place one's self in another person's shoes and understand how he or she feels, a person can only relate to situations from his or her own perspective. This is similar to 'going in blind.' This type of person can get some things right, but he or she would get a great deal wrong due to the fact that he is only speaking from his own perspective.

There are certain signs that a person may have a low level of emotional intelligence. These signs tend to illustrate a failure to understand and relate to how other people feel.

1) Getting into frequent arguments

When you do not have the emotional intelligence to communicate well with others, oftentimes, this can result in your communications becoming contentious. This is because positive communications often break down when one of the parties in the conversation is insensitive, condescending, arrogant, selfish or displays other negative characteristics that may frustrate, annoy, or anger the person with whom he or she is conversing, and this may often escalate into an argument.

2) Feeling a lot of negative emotions

Emotional intelligence is not just the awareness of the feelings of others; it includes self-awareness as well. Therefore, if you are feeling a lot of negative emotions, you may not be in touch with your emotions and what is causing you to feel this way. People with higher amounts of emotional intelligence tend not to let a lot of negative emotions linger. They seek to find out what is causing these emotions and try to address them so that they can experience more positive emotions and less negative emotions.

3) Overly negative perceptions of other people and situations

Poor emotional intelligence can lead to not only negative feelings and emotions but also overly negative perceptions of situations which other people may not have viewed as poorly. Failure to be able to connect to people can lead to you seeing more negatively than people who have the emotional and social skills to make a connection.

4) Behavioral Issues

Some people who have low emotional intelligence actually develop behavioral issues as a result of not knowing exactly how to handle their negative emotions. Negative emotions which are not addressed and remedied to some extent often aggravate things and can lead a person to develop frustration and anger which often manifests itself as behavioral issues.

5) Lower Performance

When you are dealing with unresolved emotional issues which result from a lower level of emotional intelligence, this may often result in lower performance. Emotional issues cloud your mind and your judgement causing you to be able to concentrate less on your work. In addition, these issues could be the elephant in the room in a workspace if this is where the emotional issues originate.

6) Lower Level of Self Confidence

When you do not know how to relate to other people, this can result in a lower level of self-confidence. The fact that things tend not to go smoothly, and problems tend to originate when dealing with other people can weigh on a person's self-esteem until it starts to diminish.

7) Refusing to Listen to the Opinions of Others and Their Point of View

People who have lower levels of emotional intelligence often have narcissistic personality disorders that cause them to believe that their thoughts and opinions are superior to that of others. You have probably met this type of person who tends to be loud, rude, and wrong. It is hard for this person to understand that there can be another way of thinking about things that differ from the way that he or she thinks about it.

8) Blames Other People for His or Her Own Mistakes

Everyone has met someone who has someone else to blames for everything that goes wrong around him or her. This person barely takes responsibility for his or her own actions if something goes wrong. Part of mental toughness is feeling as if you can control a situation; therefore, people who have developed their mental toughness and emotional intelligence tend to take more responsibility for the mistakes that are made.

9) Find it Hard to Develop and Maintain Close
   Relationships

Close relationships are important to develop and maintain;
however, they take a good deal of emotional intelligence to do
so. Close relationships tend to require that one person
empathize with the other, take responsibility for his own
actions, listen to the other person's thoughts and opinions,
and understand how the other person may feel in given
situations.

Just as there are traits that people with a significant amount of
emotional intelligence display, people with insufficient
degrees of emotional intelligence tend to display some
common traits as well. These traits are, of course, negative in
nature and result from a lack of understanding or caring about
other people. Part of developing mental toughness includes
developing emotional intelligence which can benefit a person
in many facets of daily life and help minimize these negative
traits.

Conclusion

Almost everything that you want to do and is worth doing in life takes some degree of mental toughness. With is the determination to push forward and surmount hurdles, stay organized and motivated, use willpower and resilience to keep moving forward toward the goals and dreams that you want to achieve. It is important before your thought processes are just as important, if not more than how much money, education or status you have when you are trying to achieve the goals that you have set for yourself.

There are some traits that are common to people who have established and developed their mental toughness skills; and these traits include: mental competency, emotional intelligence, resilience, willpower, a winner's mind, the ability to focus, they surround themselves with people who are mentally tough, and they avoid trying too hard to go against the grain. They also possess some common habits, one is by leaving the past behind and learning from it by improving the present situations. There are even some interesting techniques that you can use to let go of the past if it is still weighing on your mind. You can try holding a ceremony to let go of the past and move on positively.

There are a number of reasons that you should develop your mental strength, and one of the primary reasons is so that you can be more productive. Did you realize that people who have a great amount of mental strength get more things done? This is because they are able to concentrate and focus. They handle emotional issues when they arise so that they do not become overrun with emotion. Moreover, they manage their time and money wisely. Feeling in control of your life is another reason to develop mental strength. Feeling that the things that take place around you are out of your control is a feeling of powerlessness that can be remedied.

Furthermore, building your mental toughness will help you transition more smoothly through the changes that occur in your life. Mental toughness is needed for everyday life situations because you never know what is going to occur. Additionally, mental toughness helps a person navigate through tough times more smoothly. Mental toughness helps you prioritize. And there are a number of other reasons that a person should develop mental toughness.

There are certain techniques that you can use to build mental toughness. One such technique is to take a long hard look at yourself and evaluate who you are. Evaluate where you are in your life and your values and belief systems. Identify your strengths and weaknesses so that you can strengthen the areas where you need improvement. It is important not to allow your mental energy to be wasted on either things that are insignificant or things which you have no control over. Meditate and reflect on your day at the end of each day. Do not try to be a perfectionist. To develop mental strength, you also want to practice staying calm in high-pressure situations.

Fear and stress are emotions that you experience that have a direct impact on your mental toughness. If you have not taken steps to develop your mental strength, situations that draw out these two emotions may actually weaken you mentally. However, if you have taken the time to develop your mental strength, you should be more prepared to handle both stress and fear and continue on your way to your accomplishments.

Setting and achieving goals in life is very important and developing mental toughness helps you set these goals and get them accomplished. When setting goals, be sure that the goals are ones that motivate you. Also, be sure that they are written down and displayed in a prominent place. Furthermore, your goals should be SMART goals. Move goals into action plans. Be sure to incorporate your goals into your daily routine.

Lastly, it is very important for you to have emotional intelligence due to the fact that life is often about human interaction and emotion. Gaining emotional intelligence helps you to understand your own emotions as well as those of others so that you can identify where negative emotions are coming from and correct them. It also helps you with communicating with others and emphasizing with other people. You can gain some emotional intelligence by writing down the way you feel throughout and at the end of the day, soliciting the opinions of others, stopping and thinking before some interactions and evaluating these interactions later, observing others, practicing putting yourself in situations where you will use your emotional intelligence skills, and learning to take criticism. It is very important that you develop these emotional intelligence skills because people who lack them often experience negative consequences include: getting into frequent arguments, feeling a lot of negative emotions, overly negative opinions of people and situations, behavioral issues, lower performance, lower level of self-confidence, refusing to listen to the opinion of others, blaming others for their own mistakes, and finds it difficult to develop and maintain close relationships. Thus, taking the time to develop emotional intelligence can make your life much easier and go more smoothly.

Thank you for making it through to the end of *Mental Toughness*, let's hope it was informative and able to provide you with all of the tools you need to achieve your goals whatever they may be.

The next step is to put some of the ways to develop mental toughness and emotional intelligence in action and develop some of the common traits that mentally tough people often possess to help to get you on your way toward having a stronger mind that will serve as the foundation for you setting and achieving your goals.

Finally, if you found this book useful in any way, a review on Amazon is always appreciated!

CPSIA information can be obtained
at www.ICGtesting.com
Printed in the USA
BVHW092053190421
605311BV00002B/73